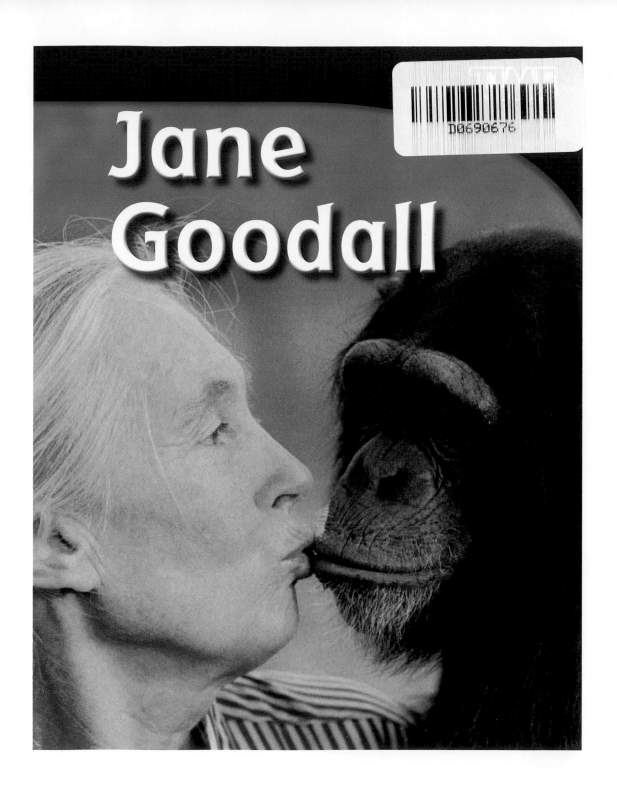

Jane Goodall

William B. Rice

Consultant

Timothy Rasinski, Ph.D.
Kent State University

Publishing Credits

Dona Herweck Rice, *Editor-in-Chief*

Robin Erickson, *Production Director*

Lee Aucoin, *Creative Director*

Conni Medina, M.A.Ed., *Editorial Director*

Jamey Acosta, *Editor*

Heidi Kellenberger, *Editor*

Lexa Hoang, *Designer*

Leslie Palmer, *Designer*

Stephanie Reid, *Photo Editor*

Rachelle Cracchiolo, M.S.Ed., *Publisher*

Based on writing from *TIME For Kids*.

Teacher Created Materials

5301 Oceanus Drive
Huntington Beach, CA 92649-1030
http://www.tcmpub.com

ISBN 978-1-4333-3684-3

© 2012 Teacher Created Materials, Inc.

Table of Contents

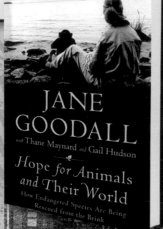

Living a Dream

Do you have a dream? When Jane Goodall was a young girl of 11, she dreamed of going to Africa. She even thought that she might like to live there one day. She shared her dream with her mother. Jane's mother told her that if she really wanted something, worked hard, and never gave up, she would find a way to make her dream come true.

Jane with her mother, father, and younger sister

When she grew up, she remembered what her mother had told her. She **focused** on going to Africa, and she made her dreams come true.

Zaire

Kenya

Tanzania

AFRICA

Jane dreamed of traveling through Africa.

Jane and her mother

Early Years

Jane Goodall was born in London, England, on April 3, 1934. She grew up in a large house in Bournemouth, a little seaside town in England.

When Jane was young, her parents divorced. Jane lived with her mother, her younger sister Judy, her grandmother, and two of her aunts. Together, they were a happy, loving family.

young Jane

Jubilee

When Jane was a very little girl, her father gave her a toy **chimpanzee**. She named it Jubilee after a famous chimp living in the London Zoo at the time. Jane loved the toy and still has it. Jubilee sits on a special chair in Jane's home in England.

At an early age, Jane loved to be outdoors and spent time outside as often as possible. She especially loved all the animals there. When Jane was just 18 months old, her mother found her in her bed with a bunch of earthworms. Her mother did not get upset. She just told her tiny daughter that the worms should be put back outside in the ground so that they could keep on living.

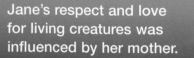

Jane's respect and love for living creatures was influenced by her mother.

Jane on her horse

Jane's dog, Rusty

Family Pets

Do you have any family pets? Jane's family had quite a few. One of her favorites was a dog named Rusty. Jane played with and helped to take care of all the pets.

When Jane was four years old, she visited a farm. While there, she became curious about where eggs come from. How could an egg come from a chicken? She asked the grown-ups about it, but no one gave her a good answer. So, she hid in a henhouse for several hours to find out for herself. When she finally saw a chicken lay an egg, she excitedly ran to her mother to tell her what she had seen. Even when Jane was a little girl, she knew that with patience she could find the answers she wanted.

Alone in the Trees

When outdoors, Jane especially enjoyed climbing trees. While there, she would sit quietly reading books or looking at the world around her. Sometimes she would just daydream about growing up, traveling the world, and working with animals. All of this quiet time alone in the trees helped to prepare Jane for her future.

As Jane grew older, her interest in animals and faraway places grew. She loved to read stories about Tarzan and his friend Jane. She thought that she would be a much better "Jane" for Tarzan.

She also read stories about Africa and the **jungle**. That is how her interest in Africa grew. She decided to see it for herself one day.

Back when Jane was a young girl, it was unusual for girls to even think about doing such things. But with her mother's **encouragement,** Jane was determined to go.

Tarzan and Dr. Dolittle were two of Jane's favorite characters.

War Time

When Jane was young, World War II was being fought around the world, including England. Jane saw war planes and even tanks in her own neighborhood. At age 11, she saw photographs of the **Holocaust**, a time when millions of people were killed because of their beliefs or ethnic backgrounds. These terrible images of war stayed with Jane throughout her life.

Going to Africa

When Jane became an adult, she went to school to become a **secretary**. Her mother encouraged this, too. She said that secretary skills were needed everywhere in the world. Being a secretary might give Jane an opportunity to travel.

Then something exciting happened. One of Jane's friends moved to Kenya (KEN-yuh), in Africa, and she asked Jane to visit her there. Jane saved her money. By the time she was 23, she had saved enough to travel to Kenya. Her dreams were beginning to come true!

In Kenya, Jane got a job as a secretary in the city of Nairobi (nahy-ROH-bee). This allowed Jane to support herself.

As a secretary, Jane wrote many letters.

Kenya is a country in Africa. Nairobi is Kenya's capital.

Sudan
Ethiopia
Uganda
Somalia
Kenya
○ Nairobi
Tanzania

Apartheid

When Jane arrived in Africa, she saw something that deeply troubled her. Some parts of Africa used **apartheid** (uh-PAHRT-heyt). Apartheid was an unfair and cruel system that separated people by their skin color. Apartheid wrongly said that light-skinned people were better and more important than dark-skinned people. Dark-skinned people suffered terribly under this system.

Within weeks, Jane learned that the well-known scientists, Dr. Louis Leakey and his wife, Mary Leakey, were working in the nearby country of Zaire (zah-EER).

With this news, Jane's dreams began to grow. The Leakeys were studying animals and **fossils**. This interested Jane very much. So, what did she do? She made an appointment, saved her money, and **trekked** across Africa to see them.

The Leakeys did most of their important work in Africa, especially the work of discovering ancient human bones. These bones have helped the Leakeys and other scientists learn about human history.

Jane talked with the Leakeys about Africa and its animals. Dr. Leakey was so **impressed** by Jane's knowledge that he hired her right then to become his assistant. She helped him and Mary collect and study fossils. She also helped them to write their reports. While Jane worked with the Leakeys, she learned as much as she could. Jane felt as though she was doing work that she was truly meant to do.

Dr. Leakey may have been Jane's most important teacher and mentor.

Mary and Louis Leakey digging for bones.

After a few months, Dr. Leakey and Jane decided that she was ready to do a study of her own. Jane chose to study chimpanzees. To do so, Jane had to go to the jungles where the chimpanzees lived. The journey there would be difficult, but Jane was ready. However, the government of Tanzania (tan-zuh-NEE-uh) would not let her go. They thought it was not safe for a young English woman to go into the jungle on her own.

The Leakeys helped Jane get her start. They provided everything she needed to begin her study of the chimpanzees.

Chimpanzee is a word from the **Congolese** (kong-guh-LEEZ) language. It means "like or similar to man."

Jane knew that studying the chimps would be the right thing for her to do. She asked her mother for help. Jane's mother agreed to go with her. They also had a guide and plenty of supplies. The government finally let Jane go.

Jane's mother (left) helped Jane work with the people of Tanzania.

Primatologist

Jane Goodall is a **primatologist** (PRAHY-muh-TOL-uh-jist). That is a person who studies **primates**, the species name for humans, apes, and monkeys.

The Chimpanzees of Gombe

Jane and her mother made their journey, finally arriving in Gombe (GAWM-bee), Tanzania. Jane was eager to begin studying the chimpanzees there. But the chimpanzees were afraid of Jane. Whenever she came around, they would leave.

AFRICA

Gombe Stream National Park

TANZANIA

Gombe Stream Wildlife Research Center

Gombe Stream National Park was formed in 1968 to protect the chimpanzees studied by Jane Goodall. It is located along the shores of Lake Tanzania. It is kept completely natural, with no roads, electricity, or telephones. It is a real-life version of the Tarzan landscape that Jane loved to read about when she was a girl.

This happened for several months. Jane became discouraged. To study them, she had to sit far away and use **binoculars**. How could she study chimpanzees if she couldn't get near them? But, one day, a chimpanzee came into Jane's camp. He began stomping and screaming. Jane realized that the chimpanzee wanted the banana that he saw inside Jane's tent.

After that, she started keeping bananas for the chimps at her camp. Soon, the first chimpanzee began bringing others there. Jane named this first chimpanzee David Greybeard.

David Greybeard was the first chimpanzee to make personal contact with Jane.

After more time and a great deal of patience on Jane's part, the chimpanzees began to trust her. Every day, Jane moved closer to them. Some of them became upset, but David Greybeard knew Jane and seemed to calm the others. Their trust in Jane grew, and soon she was able to sit among them.

First Contact

One day, Jane was sitting very close to David Greybeard. He reached out his hand to her in a friendly gesture. Jane reached out her hand and held his for a few moments. It was the first time she had ever made contact like this. She knew that she had fully earned the trust of the chimpanzee group.

Over time, Jane was able to earn the chimpanzees' trust.

Jane studied the chimpanzees and the ways they did things. She noticed that some of them were stronger, smarter, or friendlier than others. Some shared their food, and some played with the younger chimpanzees. Some mother chimpanzees even seemed to take better care of their babies than others did.

Names

The more she studied chimpanzees, the more Jane noticed that they seemed to have different personalities. To keep track of them, she gave many of them names, such as Flo, Fifi, Charlie, and Mike. Some scientists later criticized Jane for this. They said it was wrong to name the chimpanzees as though they were humans.

Jane observed that chimpanzees live in communities with up to 55 members. Sometimes the chimpanzees move to a new community, just as people move to new neighborhoods.

One day, Jane was watching David Greybeard and a chimpanzee named Goliath. They seemed to be digging at a termite mound. But Jane realized they were not digging, but instead putting sticks into holes in the mound. When they pulled the sticks out, they would eat the termites that were stuck to the stick. This was the first time that anyone had ever seen a chimpanzee use a stick like this. They were using the sticks like tools. Before this discovery, scientists thought that only people used tools.

As Jane worked, she reported her **observations** and discoveries to Dr. Leakey and other scientists. Many people became interested in her work. Her reports and studies started to be published in important magazines, such as *National Geographic*.

Chimpanzees such as these use sticks, stones, and other natural materials as tools, just as humans do.

National Geographic

The National Geographic Society was formed in early 1888 to study geography and share knowledge. It has become the largest nonprofit scientific and educational **institution** in the world. The society also publishes *National Geographic* magazine, which is known for its interesting articles and beautiful photography.

Jane Goodall has been on the cover of *National Geographic* more than any other scientist who studies animals.

VOL. 128, NO. 6   DECEMBER, 1965

NATIONAL GEOGRAPHIC

FINISTERRE SAILS
THE WINDWARD ISLANDS 755
CARLETON MITCHELL, WINFIELD PARKS

THE LAND OF GALILEE 832
KENNETH MacLEISH, B. ANTHONY STEWART

FINNED DOCTORS OF THE DEEP 867
DOUGLAS FAULKNER

"I SEE AMERICA FIRST:
DIARY OF THE PRESIDENT'S DAUGHTER"
LYNDA BIRD JOHNSON 874
WILLIAM ALBERT ALLARD

NEW DISCOVERIES AMONG
AFRICA'S CHIMPANZEES 802
BARONESS JANE VAN LAWICK-GOODALL
BARON HUGO VAN LAWICK

SEE "MISS GOODALL AND THE WILD CHIMPANZEES" WED., DEC. 22, ON CBS TV (page 831A)

THE JOURNAL OF THE NATIONAL GEOGRAPHIC SOCIETY WASHINGTON, D.C.

Marriage, Motherhood, and More

Of course, Jane's life has been about more than just her work. In 1964, she married a *National Geographic* photographer named Hugo Van Lawick. Their son, Hugo, was born in 1967. Grub, as they called him, grew up happily in the jungles of Gombe.

Jane has said that some of what she learned about being a mother to Grub came from watching the mother chimpanzees.

Awards and Honors

Jane Goodall has received many awards and honors during her exciting career, including the Medal of Tanzania, the National Geographic Society's Hubbard Medal, and the Gandhi-King Award for Nonviolence. She was also named Dame Commander of the British Empire and Messenger of Peace by the United Nations.

Jane and her husband Hugo later divorced, and she married a man named Derek Bryceson. He was the director of Tanzania's national parks. Sadly, after only five years of marriage, Derek died. However, through it all, Jane continued the work she loved. Finally, in 1986, she decided to end her research. Now, she travels the world, sharing all she has learned with people everywhere.

Jane has written several books about her work and continues to talk about the chimpanzees she loves so much.

Jane Goodall Institute

In 1977, the Jane Goodall Institute was established. Its purpose is to support people who want to make a difference for living things around the world. Through the institute, scientists and students carry on the work that Jane started.

Originally, Dr. Leakey thought that Jane's study of chimpanzees would take about 10 years. Jane thought it would only take about three years. Today, Jane has been studying them for more than 40 years!

Jane Goodall has had a full and exciting life, and she's still working hard, doing what she loves. The time line on the next page shows some of the highlights of her life and career.

Jane is an honored and *below* speaker around the world.

Jane and her husband Hugo later divorced, and she married a man named Derek Bryceson. He was the director of Tanzania's national parks. Sadly, after only five years of marriage, Derek died. However, through it all, Jane continued the work she loved. Finally, in 1986, she decided to end her research. Now, she travels the world, sharing all she has learned with people everywhere.

Jane Goodall Institute

In 1977, the Jane Goodall Institute was established. Its purpose is to support people who want to make a difference for living things around the world. Through the institute, scientists and students carry on the work that Jane started.

Jane has written several books about her work and continues to talk about the chimpanzees she loves so much.

Originally, Dr. Leakey thought that Jane's study of chimpanzees would take about 10 years. Jane thought it would only take about three years. Today, Jane has been studying them for more than 40 years!

Jane Goodall has had a full and exciting life, and she's still working hard, doing what she loves. The time line on the next page shows some of the highlights of her life and career.

Jane is an honored and beloved speaker around the world.

Time Line

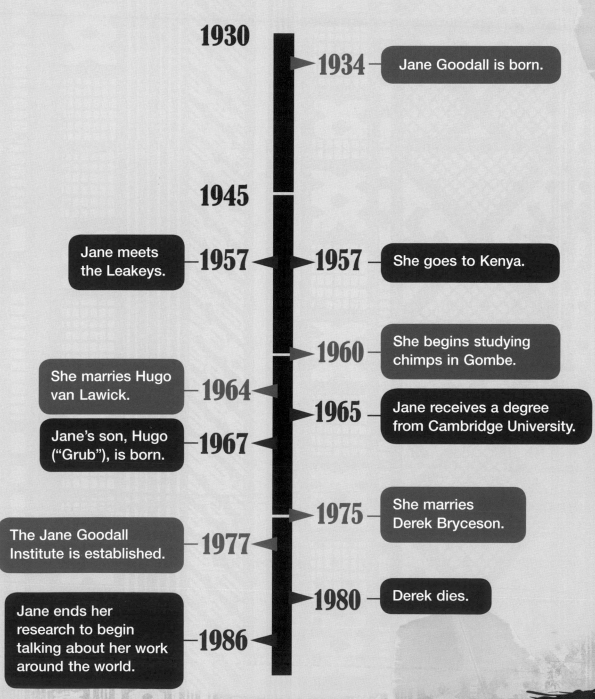

1930

1934 — Jane Goodall is born.

1945

Jane meets the Leakeys. — **1957**

1957 — She goes to Kenya.

1960 — She begins studying chimps in Gombe.

She marries Hugo van Lawick. — **1964**

1965 — Jane receives a degree from Cambridge University.

Jane's son, Hugo ("Grub"), is born. — **1967**

1975 — She marries Derek Bryceson.

The Jane Goodall Institute is established. — **1977**

1980 — Derek dies.

Jane ends her research to begin talking about her work around the world. — **1986**

Glossary

apartheid—a former government policy in South Africa requiring racial segregation

binoculars—an instrument used for seeing at a distance

chimpanzee—a type of African primate

Congolese—the language spoken in the Congo

encouragement—support or help

focused—concentrated or paid close attention to

fossils—rocks or pieces of earth with a natural imprint of an ancient plant or animal

Holocaust—the killing of European civilians, especially Jews, during World War II

impressed—to have gained the admiration or interest of a person

institution—an organization that supports a cause

jungle—a very thick area of tropical plants and animals

observations—acts of observing, or watching

primates—a type of mammal, the species name for humans, apes, and monkeys

primatologist—a person who studies primates

secretary—a person who handles letters and records for another person

trekked—made one's way slowly and painfully